AF378234

FRANCIS FRITH'S

CLEVEDON

PHOTOGRAPHIC MEMORIES

JANE LILLY was born in Clevedon, and was introduced to local history by a well-meaning uncle. Thirty-four years later, she is firmly hooked on the subject, and has an awful lot of folders of information and photographs in her spare room, as any self-respecting 'anorak' should! She has written both books and newspaper articles on her home town, featuring photographs, postcards and pottery. **Various friends have helped with this book**: Rob Campell, Laurie Eager, Alan Blackmore, David Long, Mike and Iris Wheatley, Wendy Moore, Barbara Connell, Hazel Pedder, and Derek Lilly, the aforesaid uncle.

FRANCIS FRITH'S
PHOTOGRAPHIC MEMORIES

CLEVEDON

PHOTOGRAPHIC MEMORIES

JANE LILLY

First published in the United Kingdom in 2004 by
Frith Book Company Ltd

Limited Hardback Subscribers Edition Published in 2004
ISBN 1-85937-837-4

Paperback Edition 2004
ISBN 1-85937-838-2

British Library Cataloguing in Publication Data

Francis Frith's Clevedon - Photographic Memories
Jane Lilly

Frith Book Company Ltd
Frith's Barn, Teffont,
Salisbury, Wiltshire SP3 5QP
Tel: +44 (0) 1722 716 376
Email: info@francisfrith.co.uk
www.francisfrith.co.uk

Printed and bound in Great Britain

Front Cover: **CLEVEDON**, *The Beach 1923* 74008
Frontispiece: **PORTISHEAD**, *Marine Lake 1924* 76006

*The colour-tinting is for illustrative purposes only, and is not intended
to be historically accurate*

AS WITH ANY HISTORICAL DATABASE THE FRITH ARCHIVE IS
CONSTANTLY BEING CORRECTED AND IMPROVED AND THE
PUBLISHERS WOULD WELCOME INFORMATION ON OMISSIONS OR
INACCURACIES

CONTENTS

FRANCIS FRITH: VICTORIAN PIONEER 7

CLEVEDON - AN INTRODUCTION 10

EAST TO WEST 14

SALTHOUSE AND THE GREEN BEACH 28

THE PIER BEACH 42

THE HILL 60

WALTON ST MARY 68

THE SURROUNDING VILLAGES 76

INDEX 87

NAMES OF SUBSCRIBERS 88

Free Mounted Print Voucher 91

In memory of Angela Long 1949-2003

FRANCIS FRITH
VICTORIAN PIONEER

FRANCIS FRITH, founder of the world-famous photographic archive, was a complex and multi-talented man. A devout Quaker and a highly successful Victorian businessman, he was philosophical by nature and pioneering in outlook.

By 1855 he had already established a wholesale grocery business in Liverpool, and sold it for the astonishing sum of £200,000, which is the equivalent today of over £15,000,000. Now a very rich man, he was able to indulge his passion for travel. As a child he had pored over travel books written by early explorers, and his fancy and imagination had been stirred by family holidays to the sublime mountain regions of Wales and Scotland. 'What lands of spirit-stirring and enriching scenes and places!' he had written. He was to return to these scenes of grandeur in later years to 'recapture the thousands of vivid and tender memories', but with a different purpose. Now in his thirties, and captivated by the new science of photography, Frith set out on a series of pioneering journeys up the Nile and to the Near East that occupied him from 1856 until 1860.

INTRIGUE AND EXPLORATION

These far-flung journeys were packed with intrigue and adventure. In his life story, written when he was sixty-three, Frith tells of being held captive by bandits, and of fighting 'an awful midnight battle to the very point of surrender with a deadly pack of hungry, wild dogs'. Wearing flowing Arab costume, Frith arrived at Akaba by camel sixty years before Lawrence of Arabia, where he encountered 'desert princes and rival sheikhs, blazing with jewel-hilted swords'.

He was the first photographer to venture beyond the sixth cataract of the Nile. Africa was still the mysterious 'Dark Continent', and Stanley and Livingstone's historic meeting was a decade into the future. The conditions for picture taking confound belief. He laboured for hours in his wicker dark-room in the sweltering heat of the desert, while the volatile chemicals fizzed dangerously in their trays. Back in London he exhibited his photographs and was 'rapturously cheered' by members of the Royal Society. His reputation as a photographer was made overnight.

VENTURE OF A LIFE-TIME

Characteristically, Frith quickly spotted the opportunity to create a new business as a specialist publisher of photographs. He lived in an era of immense and sometimes violent change.

For the poor in the early part of Victoria's reign work was exhausting and the hours long, and people had precious little free time to enjoy themselves. Most had no transport other than a cart or gig at their disposal, and rarely travelled far beyond the boundaries of their own town or village. However, by the 1870s the railways had threaded their way across the country, and Bank Holidays and half-day Saturdays had been made obligatory by Act of Parliament. All of a sudden the working man and his family were able to enjoy days out and see a little more of the world.

With typical business acumen, Francis Frith foresaw that these new tourists would enjoy having souvenirs to commemorate their days out. In 1860 he married Mary Ann Rosling and set out on a new career: his aim was to photograph every city, town and village in Britain. For the next thirty years he travelled the country by train and by pony and trap, producing fine photographs of seaside resorts and beauty spots that were keenly bought by millions of Victorians. These prints were painstakingly pasted into family albums and pored over during the dark nights of winter, rekindling precious memories of summer excursions.

THE RISE OF FRITH & CO

Frith's studio was soon supplying retail shops all over the country. To meet the demand he gathered about him a small team of photographers, and published the work of independent artist-photographers of the calibre of Roger Fenton and Francis Bedford. In order to gain some understanding of the scale of Frith's business one only has to look at the catalogue issued by Frith & Co in 1886: it runs to some 670 pages, listing not only many thousands of views of the British Isles but also many photographs of most European countries, and China, Japan, the USA and Canada - note the sample page shown on page 9 from the hand-written Frith & Co ledgers recording the pictures. By 1890 Frith had created the greatest specialist photographic publishing company in the world, with over 2,000 sales outlets - more than the combined number that Boots and WH Smith have today! The picture on the next page shows the Frith & Co display board at Ingleton in the Yorkshire Dales (left of window). Beautifully constructed with a mahogany frame and gilt inserts, it could display up to a dozen local scenes.

POSTCARD BONANZA

The ever-popular holiday postcard we know today took many years to develop. In 1870 the Post Office issued the first plain cards, with a pre-printed stamp on one face. In 1894 they allowed other publishers' cards to be sent through the mail with an attached adhesive halfpenny stamp. Demand grew rapidly, and in 1895 a new size of postcard was permitted called the court card, but there was little room for illustration. In 1899, a year after Frith's death, a new card measuring 5.5 x 3.5 inches became the standard format, but it was not until 1902 that the divided back came into being, so that the address and message could be on one face and a full-size illustration on the other. Frith & Co were in the vanguard of postcard development: Frith's sons Eustace and Cyril continued their father's monumental task, expanding the number of views offered to the public and recording more and more places in Britain, as the

St Catherine's College
Senate House & Library
Gerrard Hostel Bridge
Geological Museum
Addenbrooke's Hospital
St Mary's Church
Fitzwilliam Museum, Pitt Press &c
Buxton, The Crescent
" The Colonnade
" Public Gardens
Haddon Hall, View from the Terrace
Miller's Dale.

coasts and countryside were opened up to mass travel.

Francis Frith had died in 1898 at his villa in Cannes, his great project still growing. The archive he created continued in business for another seventy years. By 1970 it contained over a third of a million pictures showing 7,000 British towns and villages.

FRANCIS FRITH'S LEGACY

Frith's legacy to us today is of immense significance and value, for the magnificent archive of evocative photographs he created provides a unique record of change in the cities, towns and villages throughout Britain over a century and more. Frith and his fellow studio photographers revisited locations many times down the years to update their views, compiling for us an enthralling and colourful pageant of British life and character.

We are fortunate that Frith was dedicated to recording the minutiae of everyday life. For it is this sheer wealth of visual data, the painstaking chronicle of changes in dress, transport, street layouts, buildings, housing, engineering and landscape that captivates us so much today. His remarkable images offer us a powerful link with the past and with the lives of our ancestors.

THE VALUE OF THE ARCHIVE TODAY

Computers have now made it possible for Frith's many thousands of images to be accessed almost instantly. Frith's images are increasingly used as visual resources, by social historians, by researchers into genealogy and ancestry, by architects and town planners, and by teachers involved in local history projects.

In addition, the archive offers every one of us an opportunity to examine the places where we and our families have lived and worked down the years. Highly successful in Frith's own era, the archive is now, a century and more on, entering a new phase of popularity. Historians consider the Francis Frith Collection to be of prime national importance. It is the only archive of its kind remaining in private ownership. Francis Frith's archive is now housed in an historic timber barn in the beautiful village of Teffont in Wiltshire. Its founder would not recognize the archive office as it is today. In place of the many thousands of dusty boxes containing glass plate negatives and an all-pervading odour of photographic chemicals, there are now ranks of computer screens. He would be amazed to watch his images travelling round the world at unimaginable speeds through internet lines.

The archive's future is both bright and exciting. Francis Frith, with his unshakeable belief in making photographs available to the greatest number of people, would undoubtedly approve of what is being done today with his lifetime's work. His photographs depicting our shared past are now bringing pleasure and enlightenment to millions around the world a century and more after his death.

CLEVEDON
AN INTRODUCTION

IN MANY WAYS during its long history, Clevedon has benefited from being on the road to nowhere in particular. Civil unrest passed it by on greater roads to larger targets. Clevedon has no wealth of mineral deposits: just a few quarries to encourage building, and clay to encourage, again, building. Industries have been small, few and specialised. For a short time, lead was mined from opencast pits on Court Hill, Strawberry Hill, Wain's Hill and the land near The Beach. Salt was panned on Salthouse Fields for a short few years, but Clevedon people hold changes long in their memories, and the name survives, even though as West Lease the field was for centuries one of the great fields of the late medieval farming community. Fulling or tucking mills stood along the Land Yeo river below Clevedon Court, where hammers driven by water-powered eccentric cams rose and fell, thickening cloth woven in Bristol and brought down to be washed and fulled in the clean rivers and streams of North Somerset and the Mendip Hills.

Though marketed by the Victorians as a fishing village to enhance its image as a seaside resort, Clevedon's population had until the early 1800s consisted largely of farmers, and much of its land has been in continuous agricultural use since the 14th century. The medieval character of the settlement and its average population of 300 people lasted well into the beginning of the18th century. Tenants of the manor still had the right to use 'boot', or wood for repairs, to cut turf from the moors for their fires, and to use stone from the common quarry, Hangstone, in Old Church Road. Other medieval great fields survived besides West Lease: Clevedon Field by Tickenham; the Tynings; arable land round Dowlais farm called Dugnaham; and grazing for sheep on part of Court Hill. The mill on the sea wall was derelict by 1704, but there was a sea fishery along the coast, and the Court still had its three freshwater fish-ponds, its rabbit warren, its deer park and its dovecote. Clevedon was very much a village of medieval character, despite the fact that it cannot be described as nucleated, for it had several small but self-sufficient centres.

So what caused the changes? With the Napoleonic Wars raging in Europe, the aristocracy were less inclined to send their heirs on the Grand Tour of Europe which had previously been so fashionable. Visiting the varied landscape and stately homes of England was, as a result, becoming more popular. And, of course, the Romantic Movement in literature and art was urging the cognoscenti to an appreciation of wild landscape, remote farmsteads and the rocky seashores of the United Kingdom.

Almost at the same time as its common land was being enclosed, Clevedon had a visit from one of the chief protagonists of the Romantic poetry movement, Samuel Taylor Coleridge, here on honeymoon to escape the noise and bustle of Bristol with his new wife, Sara. His brother-in-law, Robert Southey, was later a great friend in Bristol of Sir Charles Elton of Clevedon Court. Clevedon's literary associations helped to fuel the appetite of visitors. These visitors stayed in the new houses being built around the edge of the Old Park, or Clevedon Park, on what we now know as Dial Hill.

Clevedon's growth was at first slow. The Elton family had clarified their ownership of the verge land and steep slopes of their manor when the Enclosures took place here in 1799. Initially, building plots were sold in All Saints' Lane, Walton Road, Old Street, Kenn Road and Court Lane, among others. Here, small vernacular houses were put up, largely for the inhabitants of Clevedon, who had been somewhat crushed into the existing farms and farm cottages as the population grew. However, by 1820 building plots were being marked out on the higher ground, where there was no natural water supply. From the handsome Gothic-detailed Ilex Cottage and Trellis House in East Clevedon Triangle built by William Hollyman in 1822, along Highdale Road and Hill Road to Wellington Terrace and The Beach, delectable but modest Regency villas were erected by speculative builders. Masons and tilers combined forces to buy plots and help each other out with shared skills. The market they were aiming at could pay enough to justify the boring of wells – 29 along Hill Road alone – and the building of a rainwater storage system into these new houses.

By 1840, some ninety new houses had been built on the Hill. There were two handsome,

CLEVEDON, *Marine Lake c1950* C116010

purpose-built hotels in Hill Road and Marine Hill, and the rebuilt Knapp House in Chapel Hill became the Bristol Hotel when the boarding school there folded after 18 years. The Cook family took care to move the old Knapp House name across the road to their Regency house opposite, formerly Rosemount. Select shops began to appear, some beautifully executed designs among them – in particular 36 Hill Road, formerly Marks the chemist and now The Cellars. Another early shop was occupied by Edmund Gurney at what is now 81-83 Hill Road. In the 1860s, after 30 years of hard work, he was in a position to build several of the large premises on the opposite side of the road, including Malvern House and Handel House.

Early access to Clevedon was by horse and carriage, but by 1841, the main Bristol and Exeter Railway had reached Yatton and Portishead. Six years later, Clevedon had a branch line to Yatton, and the town's growth thereafter was inexorable. Trains brought cheaper food, as food and perishable goods could be moved quickly with less wastage. They also brought commuters from Bristol and many holidaymakers from further afield, ushering in the age of the day-tripper. Farm leases on the land on the south-facing slopes of the Hill finished in the 1850s, and the Eltons were quick to see that the best way forward for the town lay in expansion. As well as selling plots, they laid out conditions under which houses were to be built, with their quality and appearance carefully monitored. In 1852, Mr A H Elton succeeded in getting the premier ratepayers to agree to the making of a Sanitation Report. They fondly thought that this could only praise the facilities within the town: the reverse was true, and a

Local Board of Health was set up to undertake the laying of sewers and drainage and to look after the roads. Mains water was introduced in the 1850s, and gas followed in the 1860s. In 1865, a dispensary opened, and then the Cottage Hospital. The town hardly knew itself.

All of the appurtenances of a well-run, quiet resort appeared over the next few decades. Public open spaces were laid out and given by the Eltons, along with plots for schools, and new churches, All Saints' and St John's, made their debut. The railway accelerated the building of large, imposing shops in the Triangle, and the old Chipping Cross was replaced in turn with a drinking fountain, now at the lower end of Victoria Road, and the Clock Tower. Yet more and larger hotels opened - the largest, the Walton Park Hotel, still serves visitors today. Lemonade stalls, donkey rides, horse-drawn taxis, band concerts, boat trips round the bay and steamer trips from the elegant pier, now the only usable Grade I listed pier in the UK, all tempted the eager tourist. The Clevedon Mercury frequently marvelled at the great age Clevedonians reached before they died. It began to be said that people retired to Clevedon to die, and then found that they couldn't!

Sports burgeoned, too. Tennis, archery, and roller-skating were provided, and later on, football and rugby, golf, bowling and riding - riding was of course available at all times before the coming of the car! When the low-lying moor flooded and froze in the winter, skating parties were got up, and photographs still survive of Clevedon's upper echelons gliding expertly or nervously across the ice, according to their lights.

Concerts were given from the bandstand on the Green Beach, from another in Alexandra

Gardens, from the Public Hall in Albert Road and from the roller-skating rink in Linden Road. Pierrots entertained onlookers at the bandstand and in the Alcoves by the present Sailing Club buildings. In due course, in 1912, a young Victor Cox opened his first Picture House on the site of and partly contained within the Curzon in Old Church Road. The Curzon is now believed to be the oldest purpose-built continuously operated cinema in Europe, if not the world. The occasional Open Days allow tours, revealing the last complete pressed metal lining in the country. If you are watching a film there, reach out and knock on the 'panelling' – it's metallic!

Clevedon's decline as exclusively a resort town began with the popularisation of air travel and package holidays abroad. The town guides of the 1950s have page after page of caravan sites and bed and breakfasts, advertised with glowing references from regular customers. There were fewer and fewer as one studies guides through the 1960s into the 1970s. Use of the car increased after the Beeching cuts meant the loss of the branch line to Yatton. This loss was more than made up for by the building of the motorway to the east of the town, with a junction at Clevedon, in the early 1970s. A ring road was under construction in the late 1960s, and housing estates rapidly covered the old fields, whilst preserving the names of local notables and these old fields on their nameplates. Suddenly, it seemed that Clevedon was at last on the map – no longer, in fact, on the road to nowhere!

Today, Clevedon offers quiet delights for its faithful visitors. Steamers once again use the restored pier, itself a monument to almost 20 years of dedicated work by the Pier Trust. The miniature railway survives to enchant as many children as ever. There are friendly faces at the shop counters, and the provision of out-of-the-way delicacies for the connoisseur. There are still local shops which have been in the same family, or run under the same names, for decades. The Conservation Areas protecting The Hill and The Beach, as well as parts of the Village, have been a blessing, again bestowed by the hard work of volunteers, many of them long-time members of Clevedon Civic Society.

There are always those who would decry the town they live in. I, and fortunately a great many others, have respect and high regard for the town where I live: Clevedon. I would never live anywhere else!

EAST TO WEST

THESE photographs travel from Clevedon's manor house, Clevedon Court, to St Andrew's Church, over two miles away on the coast. No other church and manor house in Britain stand so far apart. The bulk of Clevedon Court as we see it now was completed by 1320: the tower to the east with its slit windows is believed to be Norman. The house is owned by the National Trust and tenanted by the Elton family, who had bought it in 1709.

Clevedon's old centre was around the market cross at the Triangle. After the coming of the Bristol and Exeter branch line in 1847, purpose-built shops rapidly filled the area; the cross was replaced by a drinking fountain in 1867, and 30 years later by the handsome clock tower we see today. This was presented by Sir Edmund Elton, the potter baronet, and features his work.

The Norman church of St Andrew, known as the Old Church, stands at West End between two hills. It has many literary associations, and the footpath edging the hills is called Poets' Walk. Between church and Court, some of Clevedon's older farms and cottages fringe the road between the Gothic-style Victorian terraces which predominate.

CLEVEDON COURT *1892* 31266

Back in the days of the Norman Conquest a house stood here, and the oldest parts of the present house stand on the old foundations. The house has been altered and added to over the generations and is seen here beautifully restored after the disastrous fire of 1882. The Great Hall dates back to the reign of Edward II, and houses a wonderful collection of Elton family portraits; the Eltons have lived here since 1709.

▶ **ALL SAINTS'
CHURCH**
1892 31264

Situated at the base of
Court Hill in Swiss
Valley, East Clevedon,
stands the beautiful,
Gothic-style All
Saints' Church. Built
by Lady Rhoda Susan
Elton from a design
by the architect C E
Giles, it was
consecrated on All
Saints' Day in 1860.
By an amazing
coincidence, Lady
Elton died on the
same day in 1873.

◀ **ALL SAINTS'
CHURCH**
The Interior 1892
31265

Many of the interior
fittings of the church
were memorial offerings.
The exquisite stained
glass windows, many of
them the work of
Capronnier of Brussels,
and the polished slabs of
Devonshire marble with
their added frescoes – all
these give the impression
of dignity and grandeur
in what is a relatively
small building.

▶ ALL SAINTS' CHURCH,
The Calvary 1913 65417

This exquisite figure was designed by Sir Edmund Elton as a memorial to his mother, Lucy, who died when he was a very young child. It was cast in Frome by John Singer's foundry, and placed here in 1906.

◀ WALTON ROAD
1913 65415

Originally known as the Clevedon Inn, the Old Inn (centre right) on Walton Road, one of the town's main thoroughfares, was said in the 1820s to be the only place where entertainment could be obtained for man and horse. In later days, Clevedon's famous church organ manufacturer and restorer, Percy Daniel, lived in the house farthest away on the right-hand side of the road.

EAST CLEVEDON
From Strawberry Hill 1887 20118

We see clearly here why the valley between Strawberry Hill and Court Hill was called 'Swiss Valley'. Court Hill forms the background here, historically nicknamed 'Sir Abraham's Heights'. The large building to the left of the church is the rectory; to the right is East Clevedon Primary School. By 1907, the Weston, Clevedon & Portishead Light Railway ran behind the row of four cottages in the foreground. It crossed the Walton Road twice on its way to Portishead, with a level crossing by the smithy.

THE TRIANGLE
1925 77665

The shop on the right under the Pratt's sign is Clevedon Engineering Company Limited. At this date, the proprietor, Mr Harold Mathews, advertised 'high class cars for hire, repairs, tyres and accessories'. In 1898, R J Stephens, a pioneer of the motor manufacturing industry, produced and patented the Stephens cars and buses in these same premises. During the 1940s and 1950s the shop was run by Mr Bell, repairing bicycles, radios and finally, televisions.

THE TRIANGLE
c1955 C116055

To the left of the clock tower is the Clevedon Gas Company showroom, where the latest gas cookers and appliances could be obtained. To the right of it is Mr Denmead's cycle shop and Mr Blackmore's electrical shop, where at this date you could still get your accumulator charged, enabling you to listen to the wireless. The corner property is the Railway Arms, renamed the Clock Tower. On the opposite corner to the pub, at the bottom of Chapel Hill, Bill Bryant's Manshop competed with Hepworth's, another menswear shop in the Triangle itself on the right.

THE TRIANGLE *c1955* C116056

The clock tower was designed and given to the town by Sir Edmund Elton in 1898 to celebrate Queen Victoria's Jubilee in 1897. The tiles below the soffit and the picture of Father Time on the left-hand side are made of the famous Elton Ware pottery produced at Clevedon Court. The Gramo-Radio Company (to the right of the clock tower) was run by Mr Bird, from whom you could purchase the quartz to make crystal sets, a favourite hobby of youngsters. In the newsagent's shop next door Mr Lane had had originally run a hairdressing salon at the rear, but he took over the whole business on the death of Mr Ganniclifft.

▼ COLERIDGE'S COTTAGE *1913* 65407

The poet Samuel Taylor Coleridge married his sweetheart Miss Sara Fricker in 1795. Their honeymoon was spent here, and the cottage was very much to their liking; however, the contents were sadly lacking, and in a letter to his friend Mr Cottle he asked for the following items to be acquired: 'A riddle slice; a candle box; two ventilators; two glasses for the wash-hand stand; one tin dust pan; one pair of candlesticks; one carpet brush, one flower dredge; three tin extinguishers; two mats; a pair of slippers; a cheese toaster; two large tin spoons; a Bible; a keg of porter; coffee; raisins; currants; catsup; nutmeg; allspice; cinnamon; rice; ginger and mace'. Today a marble slab commemorating Coleridge's stay has replaced the sign saying 'Chairs Caned Here' (upper right-hand corner).

► WEST END *1900* 564p

One of the Battery Cottages in the foreground was the home of the permanent staff Battery Sergeant Major of 9th Company, 1st Gloucestershire Artillery Volunteers. The unit was formed in 1859, and was then known as the Clevedon Battery, Somerset Artillery Volunteers. After the Haldane Reforms and the formation of the Territorial Army in 1908 the battery ceased to exist. Many of Clevedon's artillerymen changed their allegiance to the Wessex Royal Engineers, but some steadfastly refused.

◀ **ST ANDREW'S CHURCH**
1892 31269

The battery gun emplacement can just be seen to the left of the church tower at the head of the Pill, its presence a sinister reminder of the fear of invasion. We can also just see the masts of coal ships moored in the Pill; they brought coal from Wales and the Forest of Dean to fire the kilns at the brickworks in Kenn Road and Strode Road run by the Shoplands and Colonel Sidney Keen. Welsh coal was first imported by the Elton family in the 1840s, after the decline of the Nailsea coal pits. There were several coal yards in the West End in the 1880s; now, coal is only sold in petrol stations!

▶ **ST ANDREW'S CHURCH**
1935 86829

The Norman church of St Andrew is beautifully situated in Clevedon's West End, flanked by Wain's Hill and Church Hill. The tranquillity and serenity of the area appealed to many poets, and one can imagine the lines of poetry streaming onto the page as they were inspired by this place. The path to the seaward side, Poets' Walk, was well named, for it commemorates the visits to Clevedon of Thackeray, Coleridge and Tennyson, to name but a few.

▶ ST ANDREW'S CHURCH
1892 31260

The parish church is dedicated to St Andrew, the patron saint of fishermen. After the consecration of Christ Church in 1839, it became known as the Old Church, and Old Church Road, leading here from the Triangle, is named after it. In 1257, the Diocese of Bath and Wells ceded the church to the Abbey and Convent of St Augustine at Bristol, because it was used by so many 'strangers', or people from outside the Diocese. In 1292, the church was valued at 12 marks, or £8.

◀ ST ANDREW'S CHURCH
The Interior 1892
31261

As with many churches, the interior of St Andrew's has changed over the centuries. The beautiful stained glass window above the altar table was designed and manufactured by Messrs Dix and Williams of Bristol, and formed part of the extensive restorations carried out by Sir Charles Elton in 1844.

► **ST ANDREW'S CHURCH**
The Norman Arch 1913 65410

Through the Norman arch, with its bold axe-carved decoration, we can see further alterations with the addition of the handsomely carved and gilded oak reredos given by Miss Julia Lucy Woodward. Designed in a late 15th-century English style, it depicts the supper at Emmaus, flanked by the figures of Moses and Isaiah. On the side wings are the figures of St Andrew, St Peter, St Paul and St Barnabas.

◄ **ST ANDREW'S CHURCH**
The Hallam Tablets 1913 65412

The Hallam memorial tablets are in the south transept of the church, and demonstrate the close ties between the Elton and Hallam families. Julia Maria Elton and her husband the historian Henry Hallam are both remembered here, and so is their son Arthur Henry Hallam, who died suddenly at Vienna on 15 September 1833 in the 23rd year of his life. The tragedy of Hallam's early death was marked by his close friend Alfred Tennyson in his immortal poem, *In Memoriam*. The lines 'The Danube to the Severn gave' and 'And in the dark church like a ghost, Thy tablet glimmers to the dawn', established St Andrew's as a place of literary pilgrimage.

SUGAR LOAF POINT
1929 82361

The dramatically silhouetted gazebo, now sadly missing its castellated roof, was said to be where Conrad Finzel, the sugar magnate, sat to watch his sweetly laden ships sailing up the Channel. He rented the adjacent Salthouse in the late 1840s while his magnificent new home, Frankfort Hall, was being built. The Hill shipbuilding family bought Frankfort Hall and renamed it Clevedon Hall.

SALTHOUSE AND THE GREEN BEACH

AT THE BASE of Old Church Hill stands the Salthouse Hotel, built by Ferdinand Beeston, who during the 1830s bought and converted the cottages formerly used by salt workers. The name Salthouse originates from the salt-panning carried on here in the 1680s. The salt was thrown against an upright sieve called a harp - hence the name of Little Harp Bay.

The sea wall here stands above the Marine Lake, made for seawater bathing in 1929, and in its time unique on the Somerset coast. From the level promenade by the wall, walking northwards, the Victorian tourist traversed the Green Beach, opened up with the building of Bellevue Road and Elton Road as new carriageways in the mid 1850s. The strip of land between the road and the sea was given by the Elton family to the Local Board of Health, and the area was planted out with such trees as would stand the salt winds – hence the famous leaning tree by the bandstand.

The bandstand is still used on summer weekends by the local bands, and it also hosts charity sales. It commemorates Queen Victoria's Golden Jubilee. The Neumann drinking fountain nearby is another piece of charming Victoriana.

FROM SALTHOUSE *1923* 74002

This popular view of Clevedon is taken from behind the Salthouse Hotel, whose chimneys may be seen in the foreground. The hotel was formerly a private house. Clevedon Hall, once a boarding school, stands to the right, in its own lavishly designed gardens of the 1850s.

FROM OLD CHURCH HILL *1929* 82350

At the south-west corner of what was the garden of Salthouse stood this gazebo (left), a building where one could get a good view from a comfortable shelter. The gate and wall have gone, though the lower part of the gazebo remains on the side of Poets' Walk footpath, which was made soon after this picture was taken.

▼ THE VIEW FROM OLD CHURCH HILL *c1950* C116036

This popular viewpoint, Sugar Loaf Point, has the pleasant, open sight of Clevedon Bay ahead, with the Marine Lake to the right. The diving platforms and the old springboard have long been dismantled.

► THE MARINE LAKE
1929 82357

Here is the Marine Lake in its first year - it opened in March 1929. The swimming and boating facilities were far in advance of any on the North Somerset coast, and visitors flocked here to use the bathing huts, the diving boards and the deckchairs. Now it is gone. There was a bandstand here, too, where accordion bands among others gave concerts. It is hoped that recent repairs will allow the lake to be used again.

◄ **THE MARINE LAKE** *c1950*
C116010

At this end of the lake is the children's paddling pool, with the boats beyond. From here there is a better view of the changing huts – there were a lot! Parents hired deckchairs in order to watch their children, but at least one lady in the foreground is busy knitting.

► **THE MARINE LAKE AND OLD CHURCH HILL**
c1950 C116027

Here we see a typical sunny day out for families in the 1950s. Unfortunately, deckchairs are no longer available. The hill rising away in the distance is Old Church Hill, where the first part of Poets' Walk led through the wooded slopes to the edge of the coast, with stupendous views down the Bristol Channel and across to Wales.

THE MINIATURE RAILWAY
1962 C116169

The railway here opened in 1952 on a smaller circular track. This train was the original one – now, the Rio Grande puffs its way round the entire field, towing the children of the riders we see here, no doubt! The eye follows the track into the picture and finds the old Glass Pavilion, where dances were held and teas served.

THE PROMENADE *1962* C116164

The northern part of the Long Beach had amusements for children on dry land. Here was the sand pit, and to the right, off the picture, crazy golf and an enclosure with tricycles and toys kept the youngsters happy. The sea wall has been reconstructed since this picture was taken.

▲ **THE GREEN BEACH** *1913* 65404

Below the Green Beach with its promenade was Little Harp Bay, with a sandpit below the steps by the bandstand. In 1868, notices placed along the beaches stated that 'no gentleman is permitted to bathe in the sea, even between the hours of 6am and 8pm, without drawers'. Anyone so doing incurred a fine of 40 shillings (£2).

▶ THE BANDSTAND
c1955 C116001

The bandstand was erected in 1887 to celebrate Queen Victoria's Golden Jubilee. Shielded from the sun by canvas shades, the band plays to the audience in the deckchairs. Concerts still entertain us on summer weekends!

◀ **THE BANDSTAND**
c1950 C116030

Before television was so widespread, on a summer day like this, or a warm evening, many people could be found walking up and down the promenade enjoying the views and air. The smart cars of the day are making an appearance here to the right. The windswept trees have now been cleared, and a flowerbed surrounded by seats has been opened up opposite the bandstand.

▶ **THE GREEN BEACH** *1913* 65403

Here we are approaching The Beach, with its Regency houses, the pier and tollhouse, and The Towers, now Campbell's Landing. On the skyline is the roof of the Franciscan Friary with its slender belfry. There is no access to the rocks now, and the rustic fencing has been replaced with metal railings.

THE GREEN BEACH
1892 31253

The house to the right is Oaklands, soon to be used as a Red Cross Hospital in the Great War. Just beyond the pier, the tall building to the left is the old Hot and Cold Marine Baths, where sea water was pumped up at low tide for the benefit of those who wanted to swim or bathe in the health-giving briny. What well-behaved children in the foreground!

THE GREEN BEACH
1892 31252

Are the capped gentlemen on the seats nearest us the owners of the smart cycles recovering from their exertions? The ladies are keeping cool and preserving a fashionably pale complexion with their parasols. The drinking fountain, right, was erected by the Reverend Neumann in memory of his wife, Annie. The inscription is now rather hard to read, but says: 'A righteous man regardeth the life of his beast, but the tender mercies of the wicked are cruel'. On the lower part of the fountain troughs for dogs and horses were provided.

THE BANDSTAND AND THE FOUNTAIN
1892 31258

At this time the Green Beach was being laid out with its shady trees and footpaths. Owing to the prevailing inshore winds, the trees had difficulty in establishing themselves, and those surviving today lean inland! From the seats, the tired walker could look across to the Welsh coast and its hills and valleys.

LITTLE HARP BAY
1892 31257

The bay was named after a nearby field, where salt, made on Salthouse Fields in the late 17th century, was sieved through a standing grid called a harp. Picnics were enjoyed on the shingle – no fear of sand in the sandwiches here! In the distance, Wain's Hill extends beyond Old Church Hill. The chimneys in the trees to the left belong to Clevedon Hall. The shelter on the promenade here was built in this year, and has recently been restored.

THE PIER BEACH

THE GREEN BEACH path leads to The Beach, where Regency-style houses were built after 1828. The land was waste ground, salt-contaminated and covered with scrubby woodland, some of which now forms the Pier Copse and Alexandra Gardens. The housing was speculative: local builders set up their wives as lodging house keepers, or sold the houses, very often to be used as small, private boarding schools for children with parents abroad in the tropics.

By the Sailing Club, brickwork now covers the Alcoves, caves which were fronted with canvas tenting to form an area for shows and concerts in Victorian days. As well as these entertainments, there was the pier, erected in 1869, for promenading and for steamer trips, and now listed Grade I. Handsome hotels were here too, like the Royal Pier Hotel and Campbell's Landing, formerly The Towers.

Donkeys and horse-drawn taxis worked on The Beach; the latter were superseded eventually by the motorcars designed by Richard Stephens from 1898 in his Triangle premises. He was ordered not to chalk his advertisements on the boards of the Pier! Hot and cold baths stood by the pier, popular when the tide was out.

THE PROMENADE AND THE PIER
1913 65402

Let us start with an overview of the area known in Clevedon as The Beach. The houses date in the main from 1828 and the 1860s. The carriage in the foreground is waiting on one of the stands for horse-drawn taxis laid out by the Local Board of Health. Many provided regular runs from the Great Western Railway station in the Village.

▶ LOOKING NORTH
1929 82352

From this pathway below the main road there is a better view of the Regency houses on The Beach. Most of the houses to the right date from 1828. To the left are the Royal Pier Hotel, the pier tollhouse, and other Victorian buildings in the area developed when the pier was built in 1869.

◀ THE PROMENADE
1935 86832

Below the sea wall here the tide has retreated just enough for us to clearly see the old bathing pool built in 1881. It was very popular with children, who could play safely in the shallow sea-water there. The Bristol Channel tides are the second highest in the world, with a 47-foot difference between high and low tides.

▲ THE BEACH AND CLEVEDON BAY *c1955* C116026

Here we can see the effect of those high tides; the beach has almost vanished! The spring and autumn tides in windy weather bring people to watch the spray lashing the houses on The Beach, where cellars flood, and seaweed is often found on the roofs.

◄ CLEVEDON BEACH
1962 C116161

The expanse of shingle is exposed in this photograph, which was taken at low tide. The length of the slipway can be seen below the pier, where pleasure boats collect their passengers for trips around the bay. The trees to the right are in the Pier Copse, a peaceful place for visitors to sit or stroll in.

THE PROMENADE
1913 65401

The detail in this picture reveals a garage sign on the building to the right, possibly indicating garaging for cars in roads behind The Beach. Despite the growing popularity of the car, there is still a horse-drawn taxi to the left, patiently waiting for custom. Waterloo House, with its arched doorway, is now the Heritage Centre, run by the Pier Trust.

▼ SPRAY POINT *1925* 77641

By this time horse-drawn transport has gone, and cars are parked along The Beach. The column to the right beyond the gateposts is the Peace Memorial, erected in 1903 to honour the dead of the Boer War and later the two World Wars. The spray from the high tides blowing across the sea wall gave this part of The Beach its name.

► THE BEACH *1892* 31254

The packed stone road surface here explains why the water cart used to have to be taken round to lay the dust in the summer. Apparently there was always rain soon afterwards, as luck would have it! On the fifth house from the right we can see the sliding louvered shutters which survive on many of Clevedon's Regency houses. At this time, there were no cafes and garages on The Beach; it was still rather select and residential.

◄ **THE BEACH**
c1955 C116008

The Royal Pier Hotel, to the left, has people on its sun terrace, as we can just see from the figures showing above the railings. As well as cars, we have a bus stop to the right, and a garage and petrol station has opened up at 5 The Beach, now a comfortable restaurant. There is a boat at the slipway ready for trips round the bay.

► **THE BEACH**
1913 65397

The lovely conservatory to the left is still in place some 90 years later, a tribute to the care of the owners. Down on the pebbles are plenty of small boats. The road has been widened on concrete piers built out towards the sea, so the stone ramp in the centre foreground no longer exists. The canvas roof above the sea wall in the middle distance is part of a temporary theatre called The Alcoves, and is suspended in front of shallow caves there.

THE BEACH
1923 74008

The cars parked here are taxis, but there were enough private cars in the town to need several garages. The car was still an expensive item at this time, and its presence is an indicator of the comparative wealth of the town. Elton Road can be seen in the distance, composed of large, 1850s houses, many of them lodging houses or private schools. C S Lewis stayed here in the mid 1920s, and enjoyed many long walks in the area.

THE ESPLANADE
c1955 C116049

Judging by the ladies' coats, this was a rather chilly day. Many postcards in local collections bear messages about the rain, but people still came to stay in Clevedon, and the local landladies thrived. The café at Spray Point had been opened by this time (in the distance, left) along with several others on The Beach, including an ice-cream parlour.

THE BEACH *1959* C116148

Here we can see the road-widening concrete piers to the left, with space underneath used for storage or shelter. Since then, in the last few years this area has been enormously improved with the rebuilding of the supports for the road and a stone facing to the wall, with arches opening to boat storage and a changing area for the Swimming Club.

THE PIER *1892* 31251

It was a local fisherman, Thomas Lilly, who had the bathing machines when the pier opened in 1869. Perhaps his son, Charles, was still working them in 1892. The pier head was rebuilt two years after this photograph was taken. By then, the Local Board of Health issued licences to the boatmen, trying to ensure good standards of cleanliness and safety. At times, this was a battle!

THE PIER
1955 C116119

By this time the pier had been opened three times: in 1869, in 1894 with a new pier head, and in 1913 with a concrete landing stage. The tollhouse, looking like a miniature castle, was designed, like the Royal Pier Hotel, by the Weston-super-Mare architect Hans Price, both in 1869.

THE ROYAL PIER HOTEL *1955* C116130

The tollhouse to the left now houses the shop run by the Pier Trust, and still acts as the point of entry for the pier itself. To the right is the Royal Pier Hotel, built for Mrs Perry in 1869. Beneath it her older premises, the Rock House, still stands. This was Clevedon's first piece of speculative commercial development, a tea house and inn of 1822 built so low on the rocks that it was nicknamed 'The Ship Aground'.

SUNSET *1935* 86837

Clevedon and most of the Bristol Channel area is famous for spectacularly colourful and dramatic sunsets. Here is a classic shot along the pier, showing the 'pagoda' on the pier-head. When restoration took place, the buildings were removed and stored locally before being cleaned and re-erected in 1998. The hotel is to be converted to flats.

▲ THE PIER AND THE ROYAL PIER HOTEL *c1965* C116048

By daylight, we can see the board with details of the last trips of the season to the left. Campbell's steamers run regular routes down the Bristol Channel through the season, alternating between the *Balmoral* and the last seagoing paddle steamer in the world, the *Waverley*. From the pier, you can travel to the Welsh coast, or to Devon, or to take a trip round Flatholm and Steepholm in the Bristol Channel.

FROM THE PIER
c1965 C116050

Looking inland from the pier to the right, we can see that there have been various changes to these plain, symmetrical houses of the 1820s over the years. The conservatory and bay windows have altered the front of one, while the house to the left of it is now the Moon and Sixpence pub. To the right of the conservatory is Adelaide House, built in 1842 and named after William IV's queen.

FROM THE PIER *1913* 65398

The view from the pier to the left, however, is mainly of later, Victorian houses. Here, the old Rock House can be seen in the bottom left-hand corner of the Royal Pier Hotel – the paler section of building. The terraces to the left of that are the remains of Clevedon's old Hot and Cold Marine Baths, built in 1876 by Robert Vickery on the site of the old baths, and long since demolished. Marine Parade, left again, is composed of tall Victorian Gothic houses, with the Friary Church just above them. Beyond the church is Wellington Terrace, named after the famous Duke when he became Prime Minister in the 1830s.

FROM THE PIER
1913 65399

This is a similar view to No 65398 (page 57), but taken from closer to shore. Here we can see the backs of some of the Regency houses of Wellington Terrace to the left. Several of them have gazebos at the lower end of the gardens, from which the sea views could be enjoyed while sheltering from sun and wind. Beyond the white house, standing on the horizon is Stancliffe, for many years a popular boarding house in this quiet road.

THE ROMAN CATHOLIC CHURCH *1913* 65413

The church was built in 1886 by an order of friars who had to leave France - they settled here in 1882. The buildings around form part of the old Royal Hotel, built here in 1826, the first large hotel in the town. There seems to have been a strong Catholic presence here, with an order of nuns in the York Hotel, opposite, and a school, La Retraite, also in the Terrace. Another hotel was built by the Clevedon Hotel Company at the other end of the Terrace, called the Walton Park Hotel.

THE ROMAN CATHOLIC CHURCH *1913* 65414

The interior of the church (which is known as the Friary Church) has benefited from the addition of pews now. The interior is plain, but elegant. The friars themselves have modern living quarters by the church since the demolition of the old hotel; Friary Close, off Hill Road, was built on part of the land to finance this. Recently a new church hall has replaced the old one, in a style harmonious with the older building.

THE HILL

NOW predominantly a shopping centre, this area was developed after 1825 when building lots were marked out on the steep rim of Clevedon Park, now called Dial Hill. Coaches came here from Bristol bringing visitors to Hill Road and The Beach, where they could stroll comfortably and take tea. A few early shops and a subscription library formed the nucleus of what was to become the town's premier shopping centre as more farmland became available for building new, larger houses.

Shops on the northern side of Hill Road were built in the gardens of the restrained Regency houses with their wonderful views to the Mendip Hills and Bristol Channel. On the south side, almost all the shops are purpose-built, with handsome accommodation for the entrepreneurs who ran them.

In time, New Clevedon, as this area was called, expanded onto the lower slopes of The Hill, and eventually merged with the burgeoning Village in the old lower town. With the coming of the railway branch from Yatton in 1847, the town's growth accelerated swiftly, and the Sixways area became commercial in character, with hotels and lodging houses as well as shops.

HILL ROAD *1925* 77664

We are looking along Hill Road from the west. The Creamery on the left was run by Mr House at this time; it was run by James Oram before, and by John Maynard later. There is a shop now in the gap between The Creamery and Perkins beyond. The low stone wall on the right is the top boundary of Alexandra Gardens, but unfortunately its railings were removed during the Second World War to assist the war effort.

▼ **HILL ROAD** *c1955* C116042

We are now in the centre of the Hill Road shopping area looking east. No 63 was Clarke & Webb, ladies' outfitters (left). Next door, at No 61, H Seeley & Co is still there today, but their other shop at No 51 has since closed. The spire just left of centre belongs to the Congregational church, now converted into flats. Note the freestanding 'No waiting' signs.

► **HILL ROAD** *1913* 65406

Now we are looking west. The shops on the right-hand side were built in the gardens of earlier residential properties; those on the left were purpose-built as shops. Challicoms were the original occupiers of the first shop on the left, and are still there today. We can see the name boards for Light Bros, 'Sanitary Plumbers' and Salisbury the tailors half way down on the right.

◀ HILL ROAD
c1955 C116041

This is a more recent view looking west. Peter Pan Tea Rooms (right) became the Peter Pan Launderette. Next door, the frontage of Dyer & Ward, Wines & Spirits, has recently been restored following the removal of the 1960s Victoria Wines frontage. Beyond are Pullin's bakery and Gratton's.

▶ THE BOWLING GREEN AND CHRIST CHURCH *c1955* C116059

At the eastern end of Hill Road, we have the Clevedon Bowling Club, which was established here in 1911, re-forming after a year at Linden Road. This photograph shows the clubhouse, which had been extended in 1925. New premises were built along the right-hand side of the green in 1983, when the old clubhouse shown here became the outdoor changing room. In the 1990s the old clubhouse itself was completely rebuilt to facilitate reconstruction of the retaining wall immediately behind. The fine church in the background is Christ Church, consecrated in 1839. The land was donated by Sir Abraham Elton, and the church building was financed principally by George W Braikenridge, a collector of antiquities, whose summer abode was Claremont Hall in Highdale Road.

▶ SIXWAYS

c1955 C116043

Here we are at Sixways, so named because it is at the junction of six roads (namely, Albert, Elton, Seavale, Alexandra, Bellevue and Linden). The post office (left) was opened on Friday 30 September 1938 by the Most Honourable Marquess of Bath, KG. The traffic island in the centre of Six Ways was the site of a cast iron clock tower, which was taken for salvage in 1941. Beneath the clock and island lay the old dewpond, which had provided water for cattle and sheep pastured here before any building had taken place. Just beyond is Edinburgh House, once used as a boarding house and converted to shops just after World War II. Pacific House, just to the left of it, is the grocery shop of R W Ayre and, before him, Charles Caple.

◀ ALEXANDRA GARDENS

1913 65405

The gardens were named after Princess Alexandra, who married Edward VII when he was Prince of Wales. Viewed from the Alexandra Road entrance, the flower beds are laid out in much the same way as they are today. In the centre of the picture we have a glimpse of the rustic bandstand, complete with its own gas lamp. The large building showing through the trees is the Regent public house, which fronts onto Hill Road.

▲ SUNHILL PARK AND THE COMMUNITY CENTRE *c1950* C116045

This impressive house was built c1856 for Peter Llewellyn, a brass manufacturer; it later became the home of J H Woodington, owner of the Clevedon Boot Works, once located in Strode Road. In 1947, after the death of his widow, it was bought by Clevedon Urban District Council and became the Clevedon Community Centre, which it still is today, much-used by Clevedon's clubs and societies.

◄ VICTORIA ROAD
1892 31262

This is the middle section of Victoria Road; we are looking south towards Coleridge Road in the distance. These houses were built about 10 years before the photograph was taken. The quarry in the background would probably have supplied the limestone used in their construction, though they are faced with Pennant sandstone from the Conygar quarry behind Court Hill. The fine woodwork on the house nearest the camera was the work of the Shopland brothers, builders and carpenters par excellence.

CLEVEDON HALL
1929 82353

Viewed from Old Church Hill across Salthouse Fields, the large building in the centre of the picture is Clevedon Hall, built originally as Frankfort Hall for Conrad Finzel, a wealthy sugar merchant based in Bristol. It was renamed Clevedon Hall when it was bought by Charles Hill, the Bristol ship-builder. More recently it was St Brandon's School for Girls. To the right, below the crest of the hill, are the houses in Jesmond Road built near the dramatic edge of Hangstone Quarry in Old Church Road.

WALTON ST MARY

THIS AREA lies north of the old Clevedon boundary, and Old Park House, once the lodge for Clevedon Park, is just within the Clevedon boundary. The old village of Walton, called Stoke-super-Mare, was deserted by late medieval times, and was redeveloped around its old church after 1855. By 1870, the church had been rebuilt as St Mary's, and the new settlement flourished.

The oldest building remaining in Walton is Walton Castle, built, but never quite completed, by the Lord Poulett c1615 as a hunting lodge. By 1980 it was badly decayed, but following restoration it is a unique private house, with its eight turrets and 45ft-high keep.

The land around the castle was parkland belonging to the Durbin family of Walton Manor in Walton-in-Gordano, which is believed to be where the villagers of Stoke-super-Mare resettled. That the area was open land can be seen from the road pattern, which in the central area follows a grid design, laid out across many acres of land which had not previously been subdivided.

WALTON ST MARY
From Dial Hill 1892 31267

The house in the foreground is the Old Park House, built in the first part of the 17th century for the warrener, whose duty it was to keep the park stocked with rabbits for the lord of the manor. In the upper room the hunters would have rested, whilst watching the park for signs of their game. The land leading up to this house is the Old Park, now called Dial Hill.

▶ **WALTON CASTLE**
1929 82354

Building has extended Walton St Mary in this photograph. Durbin's Park, or Walton Park, stretched across from the first buildings you see to the castle in the distance. This is Walton Castle, built while the old village of Stoke-super-Mare was in decline in the early 1600s.

◀ **WALTON CASTLE**
1887 20121

This is one of the best views of the castle itself that I have seen. Here, we can see the octagonal form of the central keep, never lived in, and four of the eight smaller turrets in the outer wall. The Poulett family built the castle c1615 as a hunting lodge in the form of a pageant fort.

▲ **WALTON CASTLE** *1913* 65422

Not quite 30 years after No 20121 (page 70) was taken, we can see how parts of the structure have decayed in that time. During the late 1970s, local concern was considerable; it led to the owner, Sir William Miles, gifting the building to his daughter and son-in-law for restoration. The project began in 1980, resulting in a luxurious family home.

◄**WALTON CASTLE** *c1955* C116058

This is the sorry state the castle was reduced to by the 1960s, slowly collapsing and a danger to the public. This was the building's lowest ebb, and many feared that it would never be saved. However, co-operation between the new owners and the Ancient Monuments Secretariat led to a complete restoration, using the correct Doulting stone to reface the reconstructed tower.

▶ **THE KEEP**
Walton Castle 1913
65423

The tower on the keep is 45 feet high, housing a spiral staircase. During restoration work it emerged that there had never been any joists fixed in the walls to support floors or a roof, although one of the turrets was used as a dairy for Castle Farm nearby. The Pouletts lost their fortune in the Civil Wars, and work evidently ceased near the end of the original building project.

▶ **THE WALTON PARK HOTEL** *1955* C116117

Still Clevedon's premier hotel, this hotel stands just across the old boundary between Walton St Mary and Clevedon. The two old hotels in Clevedon had declined during the latter part of the 19th century, and a local company was formed to run the old Royal Hotel. In 1882, this was sold, and the Walton Park Hotel replaced it. Guests as various as Sir Charles Wyndham, of the Wyndham Theatre, London, and Art Garfunkel have stayed there.

◄ **THE GOLF LINKS**
1962 C116160

The Golf Club is situated near Castle Farm, overlooking the Bristol Channel on one side and the moors and the Mendip Hills on the other. The club was formed in 1898, and was extended to eighteen holes in 1908, but during the First World War the course was temporarily reduced to nine holes. The family working the farm at the time were the Tossells, and their son Cameron joined the newly formed Royal Air Force as a flying cadet in 1918.

► **ST MARY'S CHURCH**
1913 65418

With the expansion of homes in what was then named Walton-by-Clevedon during the second half of the 19th century, it became necessary to completely rebuild the ancient church of St Paul, which was then in ruins. The restoration began in April 1869, and what remained of the original tower was utilized. The new church was consecrated on 3 November 1870, this time dedicated to of St Mary, thus giving Walton St Mary its present name.

▼ **LOVERS' WALK** *1913* 77662

One of the very pleasant features of Clevedon is the numerous walks it offers within easy reach of its centre. This one, a favoured place for walking alone or with a partner, can be seen here beautifully maintained by the town's authorities in 1913. The path descends from Bay Road, which is approached from Wellington Terrace or Castle Road.

▶ **LADYE BAY** *1925* 77658

The two bungalows on the horizon are Jellalabad and Vimy Ridge. Built by public subscription and from the proceeds of a sale of some of the contents of Oaklands Red Cross Hospital, they are a living memorial to the town's dead of the First World War. They were formally opened on Saturday 12 March 1923 by Lieutenant-General Sir H G Walker, Officer Commanding Southern Command. The first tenants were Privates Stephens and Batchelor, both of whom were disabled during that terrible conflict.

◄ LADYE BAY
1925 77660

When the tide was in, the bay was frequently used by gentlemen bathers, who had to exercise extreme care because of the strong currents and deep water. The girls here would seem to us today to be very much overdressed for a trip to the seaside. Picnickers nowadays are far less encumbered with hats and coats.

► LADYE BAY
1925 77663

This part of the coastline was a favourite spot for collecting botanical, zoological and geological specimens. Many a stone was turned looking for silver eels or sea anemones, and many a rock was climbed for that elusive flower or fern. The prized items were then taken home, and happy hours were spent drying, pressing and mounting them. The two boys have obviously tired of collecting and taken to the waters, carefully watched by the gentleman dressed in the full glory of a tweed country suit for walking.

THE
GEORGE
INN
A
GEORGES
HOUSE
FULLY-LICENSED
CAR PARK

FARLEIGH
The George Inn c1955
F70004

Farleigh has retained some of its village character, despite being on the busy Bristol to Weston-super-Mare road. The George Inn, formerly the Farley Inn, is still in business, and the handsome houses in the distance with their detailed woodwork are still well maintained today. Many of the old cottages and farmhouses survive, giving a pleasant, country aspect to the road.

THE SURROUNDING VILLAGES

DESPITE being Clevedon's closest neighbours, the small villages of Kenn, Kingston Seymour and Tickenham were not photographed by Frith's, whereas Backwell, Yatton, Congresbury, Nailsea, Wraxall and Portishead were.

There are wide variations in the character and development of these villages. Portishead, on the coast to the north, had the advantage of a harbour owned and run by Bristol Corporation. Nailsea's industrial roots in its glass and coal works are well documented by its excellent Local History Group. Backwell's history is closely interwoven with Nailsea's, and that of its own large quarry. Wraxall, of which Nailsea was once a satellite parish, has kept its own character through being closely linked with the National Trust's newly acquired Tyntesfield Estate. Yatton and Congresbury are both historically interesting, with their ancient farms and sub-manors of Court de Wyck and Honey Hall.

Almost through an accident of landscape, and with the backing of the Elton family, Clevedon overtook these villages in size when it became a tourist resort. However, a look at the history of these rural and coastal villages repays any effort involved a hundredfold.

FARLEIGH, *Old School House c1955* F70001

Farleigh is the first part of Backwell you reach travelling from Bristol. The name Backwell is believed to have come from the original 'Bacoile' of the *Doomsday Book*, meaning 'stream (or beck) coming from the hillside'. The village developed along the length of the A370 with a number of buildings along the side lanes.

▶ BACKWELL
Bristol Road
c1955 B564040

During the time of the late 1920s and into the 1930s, the area along the A370 here developed rapidly as Bristol's expansion meant that more dormitory towns were needed. This central part of Backwell has much new housing, but Church Lane, leading from the central crossroads, takes you to the 13th-century church of St Andrew with its oddly pinnacled tower.

◀ BACKWELL
West Town c1955
B564024

This end of Backwell did not become so built up until after the 1939-45 war. Up a side lane to the south of the road near the Rising Sun, seen here on the right, is an old building, Sore Court, which was the home of the de Sore family who owned much land here and also in the village of Claverham. The New Inn, opposite the Rising Sun, shows what a well-used road this was!

▲ **YATTON,** *The Church c1955* Y47008

Yatton church tower with its curiously truncated spire shows up well in this flat landscape. The magnificence of the south porch is due to the generosity of Lady Isobel, wife of Sir John Newton, who died in 1488; she is said to have had the porch erected in his memory before she too died ten years later.

◄**YATTON**
High Street c1955
Y47015

Here we have an unusually quiet High Street - compared with the road of today, there is little traffic to be seen. The proprietor of the Cottage Stores (right), George Bane, also went out into the surrounding countryside with an ironmongery and paraffin delivery van taking his service to folks who lived off the beaten track.

▼ **CONGRESBURY,** *The Village c1965* C234022

This view of Broad Street shows a pleasant scene of an old-fashioned village nestled round the old cross; it was not so pleasant, however, when the Yeo River overflowed and the only way of getting into or out of the cottages was by boat. Luckily this has not happened since about five years after this picture was taken.

► **NAILSEA**
The Post Office and the Green c1965 N65018

This is a rather small village green, but it was given to the village in 1948 by Miss Fanny Russell, whose family had run the post office from their drapery shop (the second shop from the left) since the beginning of the 1900s.

◄ **NAILSEA**
Summerhouse
c1965 N65023

The houses on the crest of the hill are called Summerhouse. The road in the foreground was called the Black Road in the 1901 census records. In dry summers, before mains water was available, many of the locals had to walk down here to get to the Moorend Spout in a field further on and to the left of the road here, and carry water back to their cottages on bucket yokes.

► **WRAXALL**
From Lodge Lane
c1955 W185001

We are looking across peaceful fields from the connecting lane between Wraxall and Backwell; a pleasant pastoral view, but how much longer will these fields stay green? With the pressure on for building sites, many villages are likely to merge together. Perhaps this will happen to Wraxall and Nailsea.

▼ **PORTISHEAD,** *Pier Approach 1908* 75998

The first pier at Portishead was built in 1849 in order that day trippers could land there and make use of the Royal Hotel. Later it was extended, as we see in this picture, and many of the Campbell steamers tied up here to allow passengers to disembark or embark.

▶ **PORTISHEAD**
The Beach and the Woods 1924 76000

The beach below the Royal Hotel is reached by a pathway and steps leading down from the grounds. Although all of the beaches here are only pebble beaches, they were very popular with the visitors, and boats were available here on summer days for visitors to take pleasure trips.

◀ **PORTISHEAD**
The Beach 1924
76004

The most popular beach at Portishead and also the largest is the one that runs along in front of the Lake Grounds. In the 1960s the shingle here had been swept up to the esplanade wall by the tide action, and a small bulldozer was employed to push it back level again.

▶ **PORTISHEAD**
Battery Point c1960
P90056

The lighthouse at the end of Battery Point has always been a good place to watch the passing ships. All around this corner the deep-water channel comes close to the shore. It proved to be an ideal place to watch the SS *Great Britain* coming back to Bristol for restoration, and also the replica of the *Matthew* as she left Bristol for Newfoundland.

PORTISHEAD
The Harbour c1960
P90074

The harbour in its heyday was a very busy place, with coal boats coming in to unload for the power station day after day, and plenty of pleasure boats tied up in the shallower end. It was a very popular place to learn to swim too, before the pool was built near Battery Point. There is now huge redevelopment under way here.

PORTISHEAD
High Street c1960
P90077

This end of the High Street has changed very little, but around the corner is the dual carriageway which bypasses the town and leads to the Gordano interchange at the M5. There is a great easing of the traffic that would otherwise have passed through an already busy shopping centre.

PORTISHEAD, *The Church c1960* P90098

This photograph was taken from Newlands Hill overlooking the fields; this scene is very different today. Mustad's Nail Factory on the left, with its chimney, has shut down, and there are houses all over the fields in front of St Peter's Church and in many of those beyond it as well. In the far distance today you would see the busy Portbury Docks rather than empty space.

INDEX

EAST TO WEST
All Saints' Church 16-17,
Clevedon Court 14-15,
Coleridge's Cottage 22
East Clevedon 18-19,
St Andrew's Church 22-23, 24-25
Sugar Loaf Point 26-27
The Triangle 20-21
Walton Road 17,
West End 22

SALTHOUSE AND THE GREEN BEACH
Bandstand and the Fountain 41
Bandstand 36-37
From Old Church Hill 30-31,
From Salthouse 28-29,
Green Beach 35, 37, 38-39, 40
Little Harp Bay 40-41
Marine Lake and Old Church Hill 33
Marine Lake 11, 32-33
Miniature Railway 34
Promenade 34
View from Old Church Hill 32

THE PIER BEACH
Beach 48-49, 52
Beach and Clevedon Bay 45
Clevedon Beach 45
Esplanade 50-51, 52
From the Pier 57, 58
Looking North 44-45
Pier 53, 54
Pier and the Royal Pier Hotel 56
Promenade 44, 46-47

Promenade and the Pier 42-43,
Roman Catholic Church 58, 59
Royal Pier Hotel 54
Spray Point 48
Sunset 55

THE HILL
Alexandra Gardens 64
Bowling Green and Christ Church 63
Clevedon Hall 66-67
Hill Road 60-61, 62-63
Sixways 64-65
Sunhill Park and the Community Centre 65
Victoria Road 65

WALTON ST MARY
Golf Links 72-73
Ladye Bay 74-75
Lover's Walk 74
St Mary's Church 73
Walton Castle 70-71, 72
Walton St Mary 68-69
Walton St Mary from Dial Hill 69
Walton Park Hotel 72

THE SURROUNDING VILLAGES
Backwell 78-79
Congresbury 80
Farleigh 76-77
Nailsea 80-81
Portishead 82-83, 84-85, 86
Wraxall 81
Yatton 79

NAMES OF SUBSCRIBERS

The following people have kindly supported this book
by subscribing to copies before publication.

Mary Allen, Clevedon

Andy & Sheila Anderson

Mr R. & Mrs L. Ashurst, Clevedon

The Bailey Family, Clevedon

Keith & Sue Ball

K. Ball

Dave, Ali & Louise Ball, Clevedon

L. W. & E. R. Banks, Clevedon

Walt Banwell, Clevedon 17/08/47

Andrew Bennett, Clevedon

Craig Bennett, Clevedon

John Bennett, Clevedon

Esme Binding

Robert Geoffrey Binding, Clevedon

Black Family, Clevedon

Alan & Kathleen Blackmore, Clevedon

Claire Blandsford, Clevedon

The Bonfield Family, Clevedon

The Boundy Family, Clevedon

Sybil Bowman of Clevedon

Mr A. T. & Mrs K. M. Brooks and Family of Clevedon

Michall S. Bryant

To Derek Campion love from Louise & Joseph

Barrie Carey, Clevedon

Mr Peter Chambers

Mr F. J. & Mrs J. M. Chard, Clevedon

The Cheverton Family

Colin D. Climpson

Susan Codd

Pamela Cole (nee Sibley), Happy 60th Birthday

Bridget Colfer, Tickenham

B. Connell and In Memory of D. T. Connell

K. Coombes & C. Coombes

Jason A. J. Corbin, Clevedon

Brian H. Coulson

Diana Cruickshank

M. I. & Mrs P. M. Cullen, Clevedon

Ron Davies

Bill & Pauline Davies, France

Jean & Bob Davis, Clevedon

Mr R. G. M. Davis & Mrs S. R. Davis, Clevedon

In Memory of Margaret & Ted Densley

The Derrick Family of Clevedon

Stephen C. Dimond, Clevedon

Linda Dudley and Family, East Clevedon

The Dyer Family, Clevedon

The Eager Family, Clevedon

Ruth Eastmond, Clevedon

D. A. Eggleton, Clevedon

W. A. Elliott Happy 80th Birthday

Ms H. M. M. Ellis & Mr A. H. Creese, Clevedon

Miss Julia Elton

Keith & Rita Faithfull, Clevedon

The Ferris Family of Yatton, Somerset

A. N. Figures, Clevedon

Christopher & Christine Finch

Mrs Marion Finnie, Clevedon

The Fitzpatrick Family

Michael G. Ford, Tickenham

The Fowler Family, Clevedon

Lynne Fowler

The Fry Family, Clevedon

A. B. Furlong, Clevedon

Nick Gale, Yatton

David & Pat Gardner, Clevedon

Audrey Genge (nee Hamilton) 'A dear Mum'

Mr D. W. Greenslade

Dee Gregory & Christopher Shellard

Richard J. Gunn, Clevedon

Brian J. Hall

Mike & Sharion Hamilton, Clevedon

In Memory of Pam Hampton, Clevedon

Felicity & Tom Harper, Clevedon

Anthony Paul Harrison, Clevedon

Brian & Louise Hillard, Clevedon

The Holley Family, Portishead

K. Hollier & K. Coombes

S. Hollier

Mr W. J. & Mrs E. A. Hollyman

Joyce & Patrick Hope, Yatton

John and Jenny Hopkins

Laura Horbury & Zeb Hopkinson

Trudi Howell (nee Stone)

Pam Huxtable, Clevedon

Constance Jarrett, Portishead

Darren & Julie Jenkins, Clevedon

Mr R. G. & Mrs J. I. Johnson, Clevedon

Richard Jones May 2004

To Julie love from Simon

The Kendall Family

The King Family, Clevedon

In memories of my days at Clevedon, V. O. Knight

S. & L. Lambert and Family, Clevedon

A. C. Langson

Edward & Rosemary Leader, Portishead

D. H. E. Lee

The Lewis Family, Clevedon

Patricia Lewis

Rebecca & Timothy Lewis

The Little Family 2004

David H. Long, Clevedon

To Louisa with love from Mum & Dad

Sandra Low, Clevedon

Raymond Lumbard, Crawley

The Macleod Family, Clevedon

Simon Marsh and Family, Clevedon

Mr K. Martin & Miss S. Dowbiggin, Clevedon

Joy Melhuish, Clevedon

Sara, Keith, Kayleigh & John Merchant

Mrs Anne Mitchell

Mrs Audrey Mogg

Mr A. D. F. & Mrs G. M. Morgan, Clevedon

Carol Morris

The Newton Family, Clevedon

Nostalgia Clevedon

Barbara & David Old

The Osborn Family, Clevedon 2004

The Oseman Lush Family, Clevedon

Nick, Wendy & Joe Page of Clevedon

In Fondest Memory of our son Mark Palmer

Stuart and Cheryl Palmer

Bob, Ann, Dan & Claire Palmer, Clevedon

Mr G. L. Parsons & Mrs M. Parsons

David & Hazel Pedder, Clevedon

Helen C. Pedder, Clevedon

Sally Perry

Geoffrey Pike & Denise Cousins

Brian C. Powell, Clevedon

Beryl & Ken Price, Clevedon

The Price Family

Purnell Family, Griffin Road, Clevedon

Christine, Cathryn & Amber Redman

Mark & Irena Riggott, Clevedon

Malcolm J. Riley, Clevedon

Elsie F. Roberts on your 100th Birthday

David E. Roe

Jill & Malcolm Roe

Keith Rudd & Janis Potter, Clevedon

The Scannell Family, The Hurtret Family

Julie, Kim and Lynne Sellick, Clevedon

Roger F. Shortman, Clevedon

Michael Sibley Happy 59th Birthday, May 20th

Jeffrey Simons, Clevedon

Dave Snook, Clevedon

Dr. A & Mrs P. M. Springall, Clevedon

Nick Stone, love always, sister Trudi

Brian & Sally Strickland, Clevedon

Donald Frederick Sulley

Chris & Maureen Summerell

Ken & Mary Taylor

Rob & Gay Taylor of West End, Clevedon

P. J. Taylor, Clevedon

In Memory of A. J. Tigwell, Clevedon

Matthew Tong, Clevedon

MICHAEL J. Tozer, Pill, BRISTOL

Mr P. F. Turner & Miss E. M. Hill

David W. Urch

Wainwright Family, Clevedon

David B. Warry, Clevedon

Geoff & Sylvia Watts, Clevedon

The Weaver Family, Clevedon

The Weids Family, Clevedon

Ken & Audrey Williams and Family

The Williams Family, Clevedon

K. J. Williams, Clevedon

Shelley Wood, Kenn, Clevedon

Mrs Carole Wring

In Memory of Alan Jon Youde, Clevedon

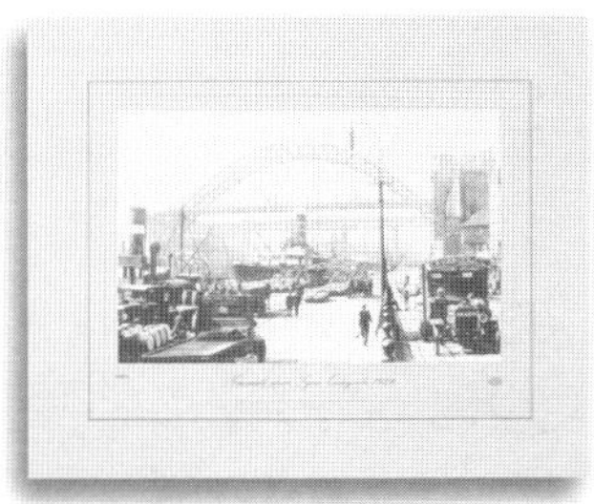

Mounted Print
Overall size 14 x 11 inches

Fill in and cut out this voucher and return
it with your remittance for £2.25 (to cover postage and handling). Offer valid for delivery to UK addresses only.

Choose any photograph included in this book.
Your SEPIA print will be A4 in size. It will be mounted in a cream mount with a burgundy rule line (overall size 14 x 11 inches).

**Order additional Mounted Prints
at HALF PRICE (only £7.49 each*)**
If you would like to order more Frith prints from this book, possibly as gifts for friends and family, you can buy them at half price (with no additional postage and handling costs).

Have your Mounted Prints framed
For an extra £14.95 per print* you can have your mounted print(s) framed in an elegant polished wood and gilt moulding, overall size 16 x 13 inches (no additional postage and handling required).

*** IMPORTANT!**

These special prices are only available if you order at the same time as you order your free mounted print. You must use the ORIGINAL VOUCHER on this page (no copies permitted). We can only despatch to one address.

Send completed Voucher form to:
The Francis Frith Collection, Frith's Barn, Teffont, Salisbury, Wiltshire SP3 5QP

Voucher for **FREE** and Reduced Price Frith Prints

Please do not photocopy this voucher. Only the original is valid, so please fill it in, cut it out and return it to us with your order.

Picture ref no	Page no	Qty	Mounted @ £7.49	Framed + £14.95	Total Cost
		1	Free of charge*	£	£
			£7.49	£	£
			£7.49	£	£
			£7.49	£	£
			£7.49	£	£
			£7.49	£	£
Please allow 28 days for delivery			* Post & handling (UK)	£2.25	
			Total Order Cost	£	

Title of this book . . . .

I enclose a cheque/postal order for £ . . . .

made payable to 'The Francis Frith Collection'

OR please debit my Mastercard / Visa / Switch / Amex card

(credit cards please on all overseas orders), details below

Card Number

Issue No (Switch only)   Valid from (Amex/Switch)

Expires   Signature

Name Mr/Mrs/Ms ....

Address ....

....

....

.... Postcode ....

Daytime Tel No ....

Email ....

Valid to 31/12/05

Would you like to find out more about Francis Frith?

We have recently recruited some entertaining speakers who are happy to visit local groups, clubs and societies to give an illustrated talk documenting Frith's travels and photographs. If you are a member of such a group and are interested in hosting a presentation, we would love to hear from you.

Our speakers bring with them a small selection of our local town and county books, together with sample prints. They are happy to take orders. A small proportion of the order value is donated to the group who have hosted the presentation. The talks are therefore an excellent way of fundraising for small groups and societies.

Can you help us with information about any of the Frith photographs in this book?

We are gradually compiling an historical record for each of the photographs in the Frith archive. It is always fascinating to find out the names of the people shown in the pictures, as well as insights into the shops, buildings and other features depicted.

If you recognize anyone in the photographs in this book, or if you have information not already included in the author's caption, do let us know. We would love to hear from you, and will try to publish it in future books or articles.

Our production team

Frith books are produced by a small dedicated team at offices in the converted Grade II listed 18th-century barn at Teffont near Salisbury, illustrated above. Most have worked with the Frith Collection for many years. All have in common one quality: they have a passion for the Frith Collection. The team is constantly expanding, but currently includes:

Paul Baron, Jason Buck, John Buck, Ruth Butler, Heather Crisp, David Davies, Isobel Hall, Julian Hight, Peter Horne, James Kinnear, Karen Kinnear, Tina Leary, Stuart Login, David Marsh, Sue Molloy, Glenda Morgan, Wayne Morgan, Kate Rotondetto, Dean Scource, Eliza Sackett, Terence Sackett, Sandra Sampson, Adrian Sanders, Sandra Sanger, Julia Skinner, Claire Tarrier, Lewis Taylor, Shelley Tolcher, Lorraine Tuck and Jeremy Walker.